www.osha.gov

I0493945

Cover photo courtesy of National Chicken Council

Prevention of Musculoskeletal Injuries in Poultry Processing

Occupational Safety and Health Administration
U.S. Department of Labor

OSHA 3213-12R 2013

TABLE OF CONTENTS

FOREWORD

Originally published in 2004, these updated guidelines provide recommendations for poultry processing facilities to reduce the number and severity of work-related musculoskeletal disorders (MSDs). In preparing the following recommendations, OSHA reviewed existing practices and programs as well as available scientific information on ergonomic-related risk factors in poultry processing facilities. OSHA's guidelines are designed specifically for the poultry processing industry; however, other industries may find the recommendations and solutions presented useful.

The heart of these guidelines is the process for protecting workers and the description of various solutions that have been implemented by poultry processors. OSHA recommends that poultry processors consider these solutions in the context of a systematic process that includes the elements described in the pages that follow.

OSHA recognizes that small employers in particular may not have or need as comprehensive a process as would result from implementation of every action described in this document. The agency also realizes that many small employers may need assistance in implementing an appropriate process to prevent MSDs. OSHA provides free consultation services to help small employers with ergonomics and other safety and health issues. These consultation services are independent of OSHA's enforcement activity. Information can be found in the back of these guidelines and on the OSHA Consultation web page at www.osha.gov/consultation.

INTRODUCTION

In the mid-1980s, the poultry processing industry began to focus on the problem of work-related musculoskeletal disorders (MSDs). MSDs include injury to the nerves, tendons, muscles and supporting structures of the hands, wrists, elbows, shoulders, neck and low back (1, 2). In 1986, members of the poultry processing industry developed a guideline advocating training, identifying ergonomic hazards, and developing solutions to reduce ergonomic risk factors and early medical intervention as a means to reduce the occurrence of MSDs and their associated costs (3).

In August 1993, OSHA published its *Ergonomics Program Management Guidelines for Meatpacking Plants* [meatpacking guidelines] (4). The meatpacking guidelines specifically recommended that employers implement an ergonomics process to identify and correct ergonomics-related problems in their worksites. Then in 2004, OSHA published the first version of these guidelines, *Guidelines for Poultry Processing — Ergonomics for the Prevention of Musculoskeletal Disorders*.

MSDs continue to be common among workers in the poultry processing industry. In fact, the incidence rate of occupational illness cases reported in this industry in 2011 and 2012 has remained high at more than five times the average for all U.S. industries (5). The rate in poultry plants of one musculoskeletal disorder, carpal tunnel syndrome, was more than three times the national average in 2012 and seven times the national average in 2011 (6). Poultry industry employers were also more than three times in 2012 and almost six times in 2011 more likely to identify repetitive motion as the exposure resulting in a serious injury compared to employers in all industries (6). According to the Bureau of Labor Statistics, of the total 3,620 occupational injury and illness cases requiring days away from work that were reported among workers in the poultry processing industry in 2011 and 2012, 33% (1,190 cases) were MSDs (7).

Many poultry processing jobs are physically demanding and involve factors that increase the risk of developing an MSD. These factors include repetition, force, awkward and static postures, and vibration (8). In addition, many operations in poultry processing occur with a chilled product or in a cold environment. Cold temperatures in combination with these ergonomic risk factors increase the potential for MSDs to develop (1).

In these guidelines, we use the term MSD to refer to a variety of injuries and illnesses that occur from repeated use or overexertion, including:

- Carpal tunnel syndrome;
- Tendinitis;
- Rotator cuff injuries (a shoulder problem);
- Epicondylitis (an elbow problem);
- Trigger finger; and
- Muscle strains and low back injuries.

Studies published in the scientific literature and research reports also confirm experiences documented in the poultry industry. A recent study of poultry plant workers reported that the prevalence of carpal tunnel syndrome was 2.5 times higher in poultry workers than in non-poultry manual laborers (9). The authors found that poultry workers who performed tasks requiring the most repetitive hand manipulation (cutting, eviscerating, washing, trimming, deboning, and multiple tasks) had a higher rate of carpal tunnel syndrome than those performing other tasks along the production line (packing, sanitation, chilling, and others).

NIOSH scientists have conducted several Health Hazard Evaluations (HHEs) that looked at the ergonomic-related risk factors in poultry processing plants. Five HHEs have focused on ergonomic factors and MSDs. At a turkey processing plant, NIOSH investigators found that workers employed in jobs requiring faster repetitions had a higher incidence of MSDs than those doing slower jobs (10). Similarly, at another poultry plant, NIOSH reported a higher incidence of MSDs, particularly in the deboning department which had the highest worker exposure to repetitive and forceful hand-wrist motion (11). In a more recent evaluation of MSDs in employees at a poultry processing plant in South Carolina, NIOSH scientists performed nerve conduction testing on employees to evaluate their median nerve function in the hands and wrists. The researchers also conducted a job hazard analyses and collected information from employees by questionnaire. NIOSH found that 42% of employees who worked on the production line and who participated in the study had evidence of carpal tunnel syndrome. Carpal tunnel syndrome was defined by decrements in nerve conduction and hand and wrist symptoms (8).

Employers should consider an MSD to be work-related if an event or exposure in the work environment either caused or contributed to the MSD, or significantly aggravated a pre-existing MSD as required by OSHA's recordkeeping rule. For more information, see OSHA's recordkeeping web page at www.osha.gov/recordkeeping.

These guidelines present recommendations for the workplace with the goal of reducing work-related MSDs. Poultry processing companies that have already instituted processes that reduce risk factors for MSDs have found that these changes resulted in savings by lowering injury and illness rates, reducing workers' compensation costs, and improving efficiency (12, 13).

A PROCESS FOR PROTECTING WORKERS

These guidelines are specifically designed for poultry processing operations and update OSHA's earlier poultry processing guidelines.

While poultry processing facilities vary, an effective process to prevent MSDs among poultry plant workers generally includes all the critical elements listed below (management support, employee involvement, effective training, periodic review of injury and illness reports to help identify problems, encouraging and utilizing early reports of injuries, implementing effective solutions, and evaluating progress) and can be tailored to an individual processing facility's operations. OSHA recommends that employers develop a process to systematically address ergonomics-related risk factors in their work environments and incorporate them into their existing safety and health programs.

Provide Management Support

A strong management commitment is critical to the effective implementation of the ergonomics process. OSHA recommends that management support be visible to all workers. Management can provide visible support by:

- Consistently communicating the importance of worker safety and health;
- Assigning and communicating responsibility for the various aspects of the ergonomics process to appropriate managers, supervisors and other employees;
- Committing adequate resources to the ergonomics process;
- Integrating safety and health concerns into production processes and production improvements; and
- Ensuring compliance with the OSH Act's prohibition on retaliating against workers who report work-related injuries and illnesses.

Involve Workers

An effective ergonomics process also includes active employee involvement. Involving workers improves problem-solving and hazard identification capabilities for the ergonomics process. Involving employees in the ergonomics process also leads to greater acceptance when workplace modifications are proposed and implemented. The following are some ways to involve workers in the ergonomics process:

- Regularly communicate with employees about effective workplace practices and provide employees with information relevant to the ergonomic process;
- Implement a procedure that encourages early reporting of symptoms of MSDs without fear of reprisal;
- Develop a system to engage employees in the design of work, equipment and procedures, the reporting of workplace hazards, and training;
- Establish an employee complaint or suggestion procedure designed to allow employees to raise ergonomic issues without fear of reprisal;
- Request employee feedback on workplace modifications;

- Form employee groups to help identify problems, analyze tasks and recommend solutions; and
- Assure that no employee is retaliated against for exercising his or her rights under OSHA law, including reporting a potential hazard, symptoms or work-related injury.

Provide Training

Training is also an important element of the ergonomics process. Effective training ensures that all employees, including contract and temporary workers, are aware of ergonomics and its benefits, are able to identify ergonomics-related concerns in the workplace, are taught how to minimize the risk of injury, and understand the importance of reporting early symptoms of musculoskeletal disorders (14). Training should be provided by individuals who have experience in ergonomics in the poultry processing industry and should also be provided in a manner and language that all workers can understand.

All Employees Training

OSHA recommends that all employees receive general awareness training on ergonomic issues. This training can be integrated into initial safety and health training. When training is effective the workers will:

- Learn the proper use of equipment, tools, and machine controls;
- Recognize early symptoms of MSDs and the importance of early reporting ;
- Learn the procedures for reporting work-related injuries and illnesses as required by OSHA's injury and illness recording and reporting regulation at www.osha.gov/recordkeeping;
- Learn about the company's ergonomics process;
- Learn how to identify ergonomic risk factors; and
- Learn the process for reporting ergonomic concerns and providing feedback to the employer.

OSHA also recommends that poultry processing employees — including all production workers, supervisors and managers, engineers and maintenance personnel, as well as health-care providers — receive job-specific training on preventing MSDs.

At a minimum, OSHA recommends that these employees be trained in the following areas:

- Proper care, use, sharpening and handling techniques for knives and scissors;
- Use of any special tools and devices;
- Use of safety equipment, including personal protective equipment (PPE), as it relates to MSD prevention (such as the proper fit of gloves);
- Use of proper lifting techniques and lifting devices; and
- Use of ergonomic stands and platforms.

Managers and Supervisors

Managers and supervisors should be familiar with the ergonomics process, the importance of early reporting of MSDs and their responsibilities in that process. OSHA also recommends that managers receive sufficient training in the ergonomic issues associated with their areas of responsibility, so that they can effectively implement the ergonomics process. Supervisors should also receive training on the OSH Act's prohibition against retaliating against workers who report work-related injuries and illnesses.

Engineers and Maintenance Personnel

OSHA recommends that engineers and maintenance personnel be trained in how to prevent and correct ergonomic problems through proper job and workstation design and proper maintenance. OSHA also recommends that plant engineers and maintenance personnel be trained in the ergonomic principles associated with the tasks the employees do and tools they use on the job.

Healthcare Providers

Many poultry processors employ healthcare staff to deliver occupational health services. OSHA recommends that these healthcare providers receive training in the prevention, early recognition, evaluation, treatment, and rehabilitation of MSDs. OSHA also recommends that these healthcare providers be familiar with the various jobs in the poultry processing facility so that they are aware of the types of ergonomic-related risks workers may face when performing certain job tasks, including light duty jobs to which injured workers may be assigned.

Identify Problems

An important part of the ergonomic process is a periodic review of the facility, including specific workstation designs and work practices, and the overall production process, from an ergonomics perspective. This process includes reviewing the company's injury and illness records and worker reports of symptoms and problems to identify existing problem areas. However, a more effective approach, in combination with reviewing injury and illness records, is to be proactive and identify potential ergonomic issues that may have gone unnoticed or have resulted from facility changes, before they result in MSDs. OSHA recommends that poultry facilities establish a two-step process to systematically identify ergonomic-related risk factors and their potential problems. This process should account not only for current workplace conditions, but also for planned changes to existing and new facilities, processes, materials, and equipment.

Review Injury and Illness Information: Implement a Surveillance Program

Surveillance for Injuries and Illnesses: To identify existing problems, employers should regularly review all reports of injury and illness. This includes reviewing first-aid logs, nurse's logs, OSHA 300 and 301 reports, reports of workers' compensation claims, insurance company reports and employee reports of problems. All such reports should be reviewed regularly and more frequently if there are any process or staffing changes. This regular monitoring should be conducted to determine if interventions (see page 7: Implement Solutions) are necessary to assure that no new problems are created. As stated earlier, workers must be trained on the early signs and symptoms of musculoskeletal disorders and encouraged to report all symptoms early.

OSHA's Ergonomic Program Guidelines for the Meatpacking Industry (1993) (www.osha.gov/Publications/OSHA3123/3123.html) also include a recommendation for a Symptom Survey — which could be an especially important tool to monitor employee health if there are any process or staffing changes. The survey is one method for identifying areas or jobs where potential problems exist and indicate the need for further investigation of that job.

Identify Risk Factors

A more effective approach, in combination with reviewing injury and illness records, is to be proactive and identify potential ergonomic issues that may have gone unnoticed or have resulted from facility changes, before they result in MSDs.

Ergonomics-related risk factors that may lead to the development of MSDs in poultry processing facilities include:

- Repetition — performing the same motion or series of motions continually or frequently. The number of repetitious movements may be affected by the speed of a conveyer belt, or the number of workers available to do the job (crewing standards).
- Forceful exertion — the amount of physical effort to perform a demanding task (such as heavy lifting, hanging/rehanging birds, pulling skin) or to maintain control of equipment or tools.
- Awkward and static postures — assuming positions that place stress on the body, such as reaching above shoulder height, kneeling, squatting, leaning over a worktable, twisting the torso while lifting, maintaining a sustained posture for a long period of time, as well as holding or using tools (e.g., knives or scissors) in a non-neutral or fixed position.
- Vibration — using vibrating hand-held power tools can increase the stress on the hands and arms. This is especially a problem if other risk factors are present in the task.
- Cold temperatures in combination with the above risk factors may also increase the potential for MSDs to develop (1). Many of the operations in poultry processing occur with a chilled product or in a cold environment.

The risk of MSD injury depends on the frequency of the task performed, the level of required effort, the duration of the task, as well as other factors. Not all of these risk factors will be present in every job. Employers, however, should look for these factors when screening and analyzing jobs, operations, or workstations to determine which risk factors are present. Jobs and tasks that have multiple risk factors have a higher probability of causing MSDs (2).

Job hazard analyses should be routinely performed on all tasks that are identified as having the potential to cause injury. Analysis should include body posture evaluation, force measurements, tools selection and their maintenance, PPE availability, and dimensions and adjustability of the workstations. An adequate analysis would be expected to identify all risk factors present in each job or workstation studied.

Another effective method to identify ergonomic risk factors is to observe whether workers are: making modifications to their tools, equipment, or work areas to address potential risk factors; shaking their arms and hands; rolling their shoulders; or bringing products, such as back belts or wrist braces, into the workplace. These actions can mean that workers are experiencing signs of developing MSDs.

Encourage and Utilize Early Reports of Injuries

Accurate and comprehensive injury reporting is important to the success of an ergonomic process. Early reporting, diagnosis, and intervention can limit injury severity, improve the effectiveness of treatment, minimize the likelihood of disability or permanent damage, and reduce workers' compensation claims (3, 13, 15). Employers have found that early reporting, combined with appropriate medical treatment and/or work restrictions, can help employees recover fully without more serious and costly consequences. OSHA's injury and illness recording and reporting regulation (29 CFR 1904) requires employers to keep records of work-related injuries and illnesses. This information, if recorded accurately and completely, can be an important tool in proper evaluation of your workplace. Under the OSH Act, employees may not be retaliated against for reporting a work-related injury or illness (29 U.S.C. 660(c)).

The goal of encouraging early reporting is to properly assess, diagnose, and treat MSDs that occur in poultry plants before they lead to debilitating injury. This provides an opportunity to evaluate jobs and tasks and ensure prompt

medical management, as needed, and allows the poultry plant to correctly identify work areas or specific tasks where injuries occur or are most severe. This information helps direct the efforts to address ergonomic risk factors as well as to guide healthcare providers in making return-to-work and light-duty work decisions.

OSHA recommends that employers implement a process that addresses the following areas:

- *Accurate injury and illness recordkeeping.* Complete, descriptive, and accurate injury and illness records can be used to identify problem areas and evaluate progress. Early reports provide a mechanism to track MSD injuries plant-wide and evaluate the effectiveness of work changes. Eliminating all barriers to employee reporting of injuries will help ensure accurate records.
- *Early recognition and reporting.* Early reporting of symptoms of MSDs reduces injury severity, the likelihood of permanent disability, and the number and costs of workers' compensation claims. It also identifies possible risk areas in the plant for intervention (3, 15, 16).
- *Systematic evaluation and referral.* A defined process or protocol for evaluating employee reports, providing conservative treatment and work restrictions, and referring employees for medical attention provides an effective and consistent approach for minimizing the severity of MSDs (3, 12, 15).
- *Conservative treatment.* If provided early in the development of an MSD, conservative treatment may eliminate the need for more invasive medical procedures. Conservative treatment may include rest, hot or cold therapy, nonsteroidal anti-inflammatory agents, exercise, or night splints, depending on the nature and severity of the problem (3, 11, 16).
- *Conservative return-to-work (restricted duty).* Modified or restricted work, job accommodations or light duty for a worker with an MSD, can allow the worker to continue to perform productive work for the employer while continuing to allow recovery from injury. Some MSDs require weeks (or months, in rare cases) of restricted work to allow for complete recovery (3, 15, 16).

- *Systematic monitoring of employees' health.* Monitoring employee health will help to prevent MSDs. Employers should consider instituting a medical surveillance program for musculoskeletal disorders to monitor employee health and determine the effectiveness of exposure prevention and medical management strategies. The following source provides information on medical monitoring and surveillance (www.osha.gov/Publications/OSHA3123/3123.html; (8)).

- *Additional use of medical resources.* Health-care professionals play a number of important roles as ergonomic team members. Systematic follow-up of employee reports of injury provides an opportunity to reinforce good work practices, modify conservative treatment plans, adjust work restrictions, or refer the employee for medical attention (3, 15, 16). Some poultry processing facilities employ a healthcare professional with training in the prevention and treatment of MSDs to receive and address reports of injuries. Employing healthcare professionals, and/or establishing permanent relationships with outside health-care professionals, allows the employer to quickly and effectively respond to employee reports of injury, evaluate employees, make medical referral recommendations, provide treatment and monitor the recovery of injured employees. OSHA recommends that these healthcare providers, at a minimum, conduct periodic, systematic workplace walkthroughs to remain knowledgeable about operations and work practices at the workplace, to identify potential light duty jobs and to maintain close contact with the employees. A healthcare professional's knowledge of the facility will allow him or her to assist the injured worker during the healing process and in post-injury work placement (3, 15).

- *Training.* Early reporting of signs and symptoms of MSDs and conservative return to work programs is particularly important. Training should encourage employees to report early indications of MSDs before more serious MSDs develop.

Implement Solutions

The number and severity of MSDs resulting from exposure to the identified risk factors, as well as their associated costs, can be substantially reduced by implementing changes in the workplace that are based on sound ergonomic principles (1).

Ergonomic solutions for poultry processing include engineering changes to workstations and equipment, administrative actions, work practices, and personal protective equipment (PPE). The recommended solutions presented on the following pages are not intended to be an exhaustive list, nor does OSHA expect that all of them will be used in any given facility. Poultry processing facilities are encouraged to develop innovative ergonomic solutions that are appropriate to their facilities. OSHA recommends that employers use engineering solutions where feasible as the preferred method of preventing MSDs in poultry processing facilities.

Poultry processors may need to modify workstations, purchase equipment, or change work practices to achieve their ergonomic goals. Simple, low-cost solutions are often available to solve problems. Employers should consider ergonomic issues when designing new plants or redesigning existing plants, when major changes are easier to implement, and ergonomic design elements can be incorporated at little or no additional cost.

Examples of engineering controls include installing work tables that adjust to various heights and load levels or removing a section of work surface to allow the employee to get closer to items located at the workstation. Another example is fixing the location of sharpeners on shelves so that they do not require reaching above the shoulders. Additional examples are found in the *Engineering Solutions* section of this guidance document.

Many poultry processors have found that administrative solutions can also be used to reduce the duration and frequency of exposure to risk factors. The following are some examples of administrative solutions used effectively by poultry processors:

- Institute a sharpening and maintenance program that ensures that knives, scissors and other tools used for cutting are sharp. Using dull knives or other cutting tools result in workers having to apply more force than necessary to get the job done.
- Use a rotation schedule to address high-risk tasks (e.g., using vibrating hand tools or deboning activities) or to minimize exposure to cold. Design a job rotation schedule in which workers rotate between jobs that use different muscle groups. Job rotation may alleviate physical fatigue and stress to a particular set of muscles and tendons. To set up a job rotation system, employers should consider the nature and extent of exertions and the body parts used for each task. A job rotation system between different tasks is created to reduce exposure to any single risk factor and to allow body parts to either rest completely, work at slower rates, use less force, or work in more neutral postures. It is important in any rotation to monitor employee reports of symptoms to assure that the rotation is not aggravating a problem.
- Staffing "floaters" provides periodic breaks between scheduled breaks.
- New employees, reassigned employees, and employees returning from an extended time off for vacation or some other purpose often will need a conditioning or break-in period to get them accustomed to an activity and strengthen them for the physically demanding work they will be performing. Employees new to a task should be assigned to an experienced trainer for job training and evaluation during the conditioning period. Employers should assign enough trainers to provide the necessary training, especially for new employees and employees moved to jobs to which they are not accustomed.
- Allow pauses to rest fatigued muscles.
- When employees work in a cold environment, employers should limit exposure to cold by providing a warm, dry break area and allowing frequent, short breaks to let workers warm up.

It is also important to use appropriate clothing and personal protective equipment when working in cold environments. When combined with exposure to other risk factors, cold can increase the risk of developing an MSD.

- Cross-train employees so that sufficient support is available for peak production, to cover breaks, and to institute job enlargement programs.
- Perform routine and preventive maintenance on a schedule to assure that the equipment is working properly.

OSHA recommends that employers train employees on:

- proper use and maintenance of pneumatic and power tools;
- knife sharpening and maintenance schedules; good cutting techniques;
- proper lifting techniques;
- use and maintenance of effective PPE (for example, good fitting thermal gloves can help with cold conditions while maintaining the ability to grasp items easily); and
- proper set-up of adjustable stands; provide specific information about working height recommendations;

Evaluate Progress

The main purpose of implementing an ergonomics program is to prevent MSDs and improve worker health. Procedures and mechanisms to evaluate the implementation of the ergonomics process and to monitor progress are also important. Evaluation and follow-up are central to continuous improvement and long-term success. OSHA recommends that the MSD prevention process be regularly evaluated to determine whether it is meeting its goals and objectives. Such evaluations should include input from managers, supervisors, and employees who review the goals and objectives identified, suggest changes in the process, and evaluate the effectiveness of implemented solutions.

Employers should consider instituting a medical surveillance program for musculoskeletal disorders to monitor employee health and determine the effectiveness of exposure prevention and medical management strategies.

As an MSD prevention process matures, assessments should include:

■ Determining whether initial goals set for the ergonomic process have been met;

■ Determining the success of the implemented ergonomic solutions;

■ Evaluating objective measures, such as whether:
   — The time between hazard identification and implementation of appropriate solutions has been reduced;
   — The number of jobs analyzed and risk factors reduced or eliminated has increased;
   — More workers have been trained on preventing MSDs;

■ Reviewing facility first-aid reports, injury trends, workers' compensation cases, absenteeism rates, job transfer requests, or other similar indicators to determine if ergonomics-related efforts have made an impact; and

■ Obtaining feedback from workers, supervisors, and healthcare professionals regarding any change in their understanding of ergonomics, their enthusiasm or acceptance of their facility's ergonomics process, and workers' attitudes toward their own safety.

For more established MSD prevention processes, evaluations should focus on long-term trends, such as changes in:

■ Injury and illness rates;

■ The number of OSHA-recordable MSDs or the facility's MSD incident rate, or the facility severity rate;

■ The number of first-aid reports or visits to a health clinic;

■ Workers' compensation claims and the average workers' compensation costs per MSD;

■ Medical costs associated with work-related MSDs;

■ Quality of product produced;

■ Reduction in turnover and complaints; and

■ Job satisfaction indicators.

Facilities should use the findings from an ergonomic process evaluation to modify process goals, establish new priorities, and integrate the ergonomics process into the company's overall business plan.

Employers should consider seeking the consultation of an occupational health professional trained in ergonomics for assistance in one or more components of this process if and when company initiatives do not adequately address an issue. OSHA Consultation services are free to small businesses. For more information, see page 28.

ENGINEERING SOLUTIONS

Many poultry processors have successfully implemented engineering ergonomic solutions in their facilities as a way to address their workers' MSD injury risks. The solutions on the following pages are not intended to be an exhaustive list and are only examples of some successful interventions. Individual poultry processing facilities should try to use these ideas as a starting point as they look for other innovative methods that will meet their facility's needs.

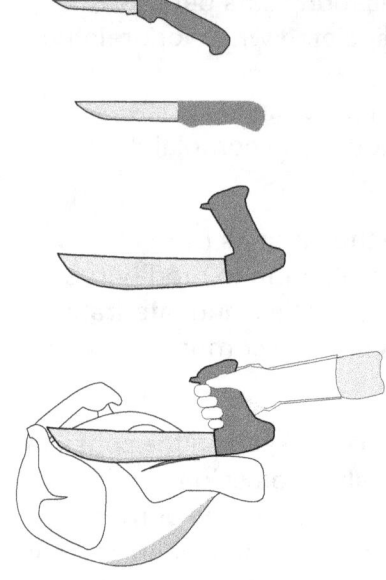

DESCRIPTION:

Designs of hand tools such as knives, pliers, and scissors that minimize bending of the wrist either side-to-side or up and down and minimize the finger force and contact stress to fingers and the palm.

WHEN TO USE:

For all hand tool applications especially those that are used repeatedly or for long periods of time.

POINTS TO REMEMBER:

To maintain neutral wrist postures:

- Handles should be perpendicular to the line of action, extend at least the length of the palm, and have a non-slip surface.
- Angled and pistol grip handles help keep the wrist in a neutral posture while performing slicing-type cuts.
- When used with an angled cutting surface a handle with about a 45 degree bend will minimize wrist bending.
- In-line handles are best for stabbing-type cuts where the tip of the knife is used to perform the cut.

To minimize finger force:

- Handles should help prevent transmission of cold and vibration from the tool to the hand.
- Handles should be of an adequate diameter to allow the use of a power grip but should not be too big for smaller workers. Generally, the hand should be able to maintain a "C" shape between the fingers and thumb.
- A wraparound handle or strap allows the worker to maintain control of the tool while relaxing the fingers on the handle.
- A handle guard may be added to certain tools to prevent the hand from slipping forward onto the blade.
- Textured handles improve grip, reduce hand force, and should be cleaned to maintain friction.
- If heavy tools are used, they may need to have two handles so they can be used with both hands or be suspended or counterbalanced.
- Knife blades that are longer than necessary for the task require more finger force exertion to perform the task. Use a knife that is sized and designed for the task performed.

To minimize contact stress to the palms and fingers:

- Avoid concentrated pressure on small parts of the fingers (e.g., forceful opening of scissors) by using spring-loaded scissors or shears or padding contact points.
- Ensure that handles extend across the entire hand. Handles that are too short can press into the palm of the hand.

DESCRIPTION:
Selection of powered and manual tools for cutting, deboning, and other operations can reduce finger force and encourage neutral postures.

WHEN TO USE:
For nearly all tasks in poultry processing, including evisceration, venting, deboning, filleting, peeling gizzards, and separation of internal organs.

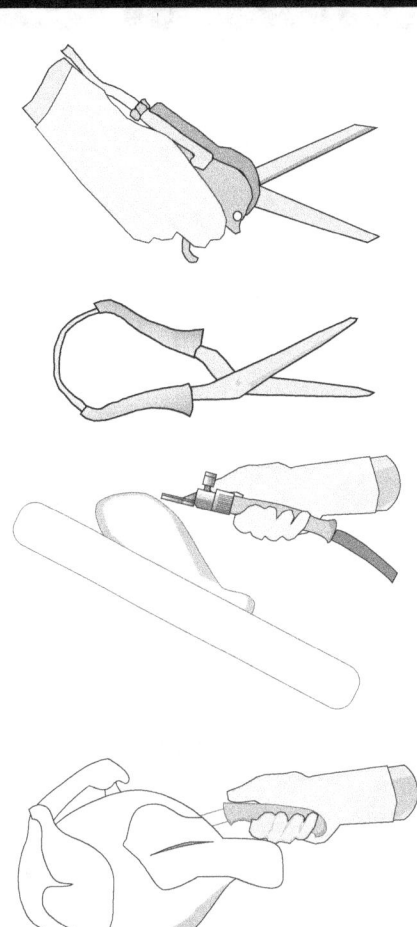

POINTS TO REMEMBER:
- Hand tools should be selected so that the handle angle allows the wrist to work in a neutral posture.
- Powered hand tools must adhere to the same principles of sizing and orientation recommended for manual tools.
- Spring-loaded handles eliminate thumb force required to open blades for sequential cuts.
- Spring force should be designed to minimize hand fatigue.
- A bench-mounted circular or electric saw is effective for cutting whole birds and breasts in half and allows the worker to use less finger force and maintain more neutral postures.
- Powered (pneumatic) or spring-loaded shears and circular knives or manual knives are preferred for cutting smaller parts (e.g., trimming and eviscerating).
- Shears are preferred for heart and liver separation from the rest of the viscera.
- A specialized tool has been developed for cleaning gizzards (a powered hand-held device with a small bladed wheel).
- A thigh popper that operates in an in-line orientation reduces required hand forces when compared to the traditional manual technique.

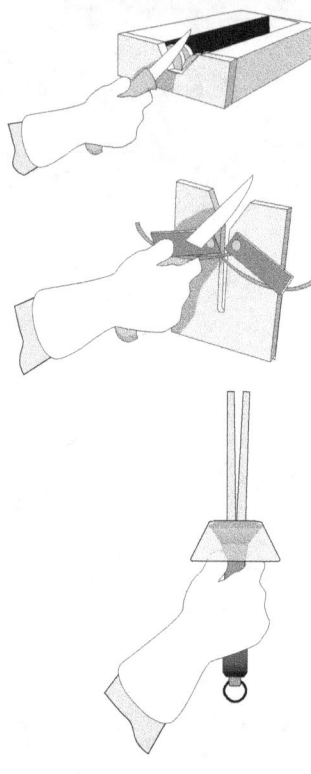

DESCRIPTION:

Procedures for maintaining knives, saws, and scissors in optimal functioning condition.

WHEN TO USE:

For working with knives, saws, and scissors.

POINTS TO REMEMBER:

- Implement knife-sharpening and maintenance program to assure that knives, scissors, and other tools used for cutting are sharp.
- The sharper the edge, the lower the force (and possibly repetitions) required to complete the task. Sharpening blades is a highly skilled task that requires specialized training. Options for maintaining a sharp edge include having several knives assigned to a worker, trading out knives quickly and easily, and keeping the blade free of metal fragments or burrs.
- Keeping the blade free of burrs requires constant attention. Workers may be taught to manually "steel" or use a mousetrap sharpener for deburring. Manual steeling is a two-handed operation requiring the worker to hold the honing mechanism in one hand and a knife in the other, both unsupported.
- A customized tool can be developed that has one straight handle and two in-line steels positioned to ensure that the knife contacts both steels evenly. The mousetrap (with attached honing mechanism) is fixed to a stationary surface (such as a table or rail) or portable surface (such as a scabbard) and requires only a one-handed operation.
- Whizard® knives should be sharpened with a dedicated device designed for sharpening rotary knife blades.
- Whizard® knives should be steeled with a dedicated steeling device designed for the tool. A standard, long-sharpening steel will not impart an edge that is at the right angle on the inside and outside of the blade.
- Deburr or change knives if product damage becomes apparent, an increase in muscle force is required, or if the blade contacts bone, chain-mail glove, or other hard objects.
- Grinding wheels may break up and eject. Bits and pieces of metal and stone may be thrown off during sharpening. Workers should wear safety goggles or other protective eyewear and use only grinding wheels with rpm rating matching the spindle speed of the grinder. It is recommended to check for non-visible damage to the grinding wheel and to follow manufacturer's recommendations for guarding and use of the grinding wheel.
- The sharpeners should be placed in locations that do not require reaching above the shoulder to use them (8).

DESCRIPTION:
Designs that minimize hand force and keep the wrist in a straight posture.

WHEN TO USE:
For all sanitation operations using spray nozzles for long periods.

POINTS TO REMEMBER:

- Avoid single finger activation, especially using the index finger.
- Investigate options for hand actuators that are compatible with the shape, width, and size of the hand.
- Provide swivel handles for hoses such as those used for water which are hand-held.
- Provide pistol grip handles for hand spraying using high-pressure hoses.
- Use the entire finger rather than just the fingertip to activate the trigger, minimizing tendon irritation.

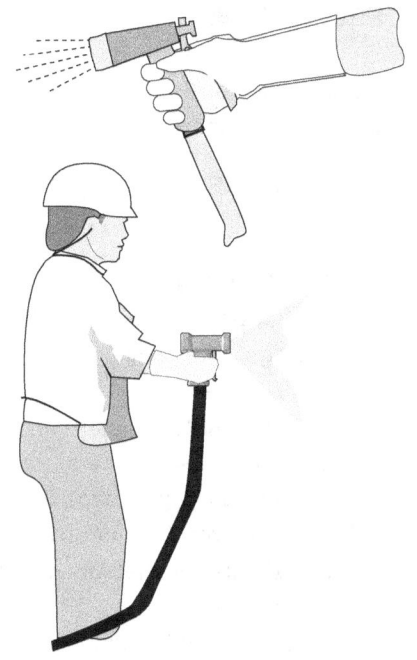

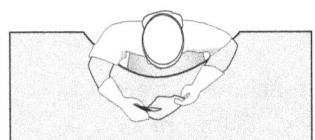

DESCRIPTION:
Removal of a section of work surface to allow the employee to get closer to items located at the workstation.

WHEN TO USE:
Where excessive leaning or reaching is required to access material at a workstation, especially if material is brought to the workstation by conveyors.

POINTS TO REMEMBER:

- Placing items closer to the worker minimizes excessive reaching and bending. Maximum reach should not exceed an arm's length with the torso upright. Ideally, workers should be able to access product while keeping the elbows in close to the body.
- Remember that it may also be necessary to provide more space for the knees and feet when providing a cutout in the work surface. If space is not also created under the cutout workers cannot move forward for better access.
- Providing cutouts can increase the amount of useable space for placement of poultry parts, tools, supplies, and other items.
- Ensure that workstation edges are rounded to avoid discomfort from direct arm contact.

DESCRIPTION:

Mechanisms and fixtures used to minimize manual handling of product by placing whole birds or poultry products into packaging, and packages into shipping containers.

WHEN TO USE:

When packaging finished product.

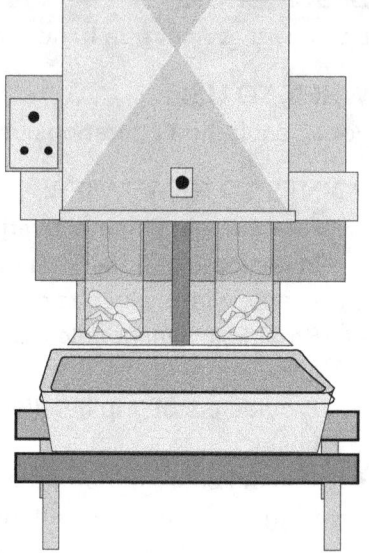

POINTS TO REMEMBER:

- Auto baggers allow whole birds or parts to be pushed or dropped into bags. These systems may automatically count or weigh parts for inventory needs.
- Semi-automated systems may require manual placement of the bag while products drop or slide into the bag, and may use a stream of air to automatically open bags in preparation for loading.
- Filled bags may be automatically crimped or fastened closed.
- Many semi-automated systems are designed to allow workers to alternate hands.
- A hoist system is recommended to load rolls of plastic film.
- If a hand scoop is used to collect loose product such as gizzards, livers, or hearts, it should have a bent handle to keep the wrist in a neutral posture. The handle should be rubber or roughened plastic for easier grip.
- Packaged meats may be dropped directly into packing boxes and then sent to autosealers for sealing, labeling, and palletizing.

DESCRIPTION:

Mechanical device that tilts or inverts a container in order to dump or improve access to its contents. These devices reduce bending and reaching to remove product from tubs.

WHEN TO USE:

For unloading the contents of a container into a machine, different container, waste receptacle, conveyor, or onto a workstation.

POINTS TO REMEMBER:

- May eliminate the need for shoveling, especially for ice.
- The position of the tilter or dumper can be adjusted to minimize bending and reaching to access items in the container.
- Use wheeled carts or tubs to move products to the tilter or dumper or tilters and dumpers can be placed on wheels so they can be moved to different parts of the work floor.

DESCRIPTION:
Tunnel-type mechanism attached to a hole in the workstation surface into which poultry parts or other items can be dropped and transported.

WHEN TO USE:
For transport of separated poultry parts or other items. Items may drop directly to a container, conveyor, auger, or into a vacuum system for transport.

POINTS TO REMEMBER:
- Chute openings should be appropriate to the size of the part handled, so it does not interfere with the processing task, and does not require excessive force to push the parts into the chute.
- Chutes should be placed so they do not interfere with the task being performed but close enough so workers can access them with minimal reaching and bending. Maximum reach should not exceed arm's length with the torso upright.

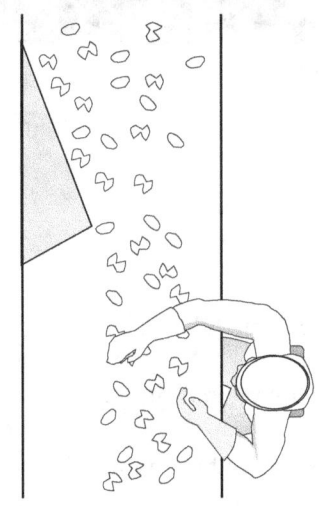

DESCRIPTION:
Mechanical barrier that directs material on a conveyor or slide.

WHEN TO USE:
Where excessive leaning or reaching is required to access material on the far side of a conveyor or slide.

POINTS TO REMEMBER:
- Delivering and placing parts closer to the worker minimizes reaching and bending. Maximum reach should not exceed arm's length with the torso upright.
- Can be adjusted to split poultry parts delivery onto either side of a conveyor, slide, or work area so that employees can work on both sides of the line.

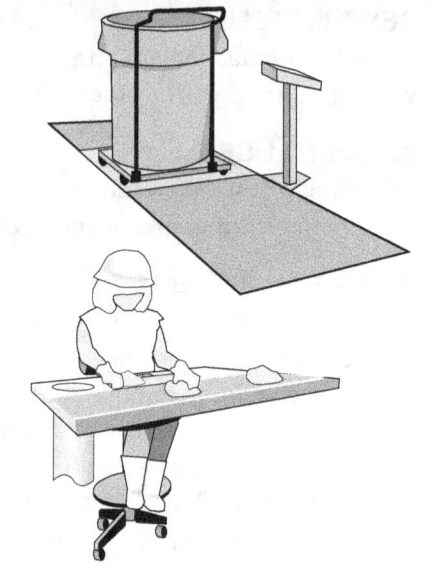

DESCRIPTION:
Embedded scales that incorporate weighing into the production process to eliminate unnecessary handling of poultry, poultry parts, processed meats, and waste.

WHEN TO USE:
When operations require that materials be weighed.

POINTS TO REMEMBER:
- A scale can be recessed into the floor so that carts can be rolled onto it for weighing without pushing carts uphill.
- Locate scales within easy reach, in the work area rather than at another work area behind the employee. Recess the scale to the same height as the countertop so that poultry can be placed on and removed from the scale without lifting.
- For boxed goods, a scale incorporated into the packing station can determine weight during initial loading and eliminate reweighing later.
- Scales can also be incorporated into conveyor and shackle systems.

DESCRIPTION:
Mechanical devices used to position and transport poultry for processing.

WHEN TO USE:
In all hanging processes.

POINTS TO REMEMBER:
- Automatic rehangers can reduce multiple lifting associated with hanging birds.
- Provide a rack or other support surface to hold the weight of the bird so that the legs can be easily placed into the shackles.
- Ensure that shackle length is appropriate to the size of bird handled to minimize the need for rehanging. A shackle which is too long may allow the bird to come unhooked from the shackle.
- Consider a rail or guide bar behind the birds to minimize bird movement and reaching by workers.
- Orient shackles or work stands so workers have access with minimal forward reach and no trunk twisting.
- Design the conveyor system to move the legs toward the shackle for easy placement into the shackle while supporting the weight of the bird. Preferably, the bird and shackles are automatically aligned.
- Provide adequate spacing between shackles to prevent birds from tangling. Adequate spacing of shackles may reduce rework and the need to separate birds.

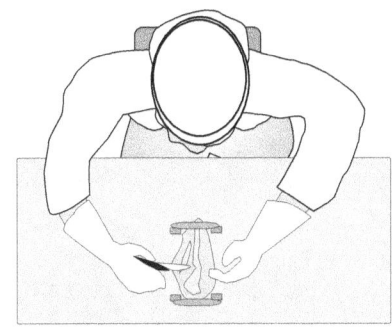

DESCRIPTION:
Mechanical devices used to position and stabilize poultry parts for processing.

WHEN TO USE:
In cutting and deboning operations where proper positioning of the product will minimize excessive use of force or awkward postures.

POINTS TO REMEMBER:
- Use a clamping device to hold the bird's breast securely when cutting or deboning, ensuring that the device does not damage the product. Once the bird has been stabilized, the worker is able to use a 2-handed method to pull meat off the bone. The device may be of mechanical or vacuum design.
- Clamps reduce gripping with the non-cutting hand. Height adjustability within the clamp allows the worker to work without awkward arm postures. Devices should be adjustable to at least 2 different angles to allow an in-line knife to be used without awkward arm postures.
- Use cones or cutting blocks that can be adjusted to minimize the reach of the arms and the deviation of the wrists.
- For tendon removal, the tip of the tendon can be placed into a vise that uses a mechanical arm to pull and separate it from the meat, leaving the meat in good condition. The vise reduces holding and pinching with the hand.

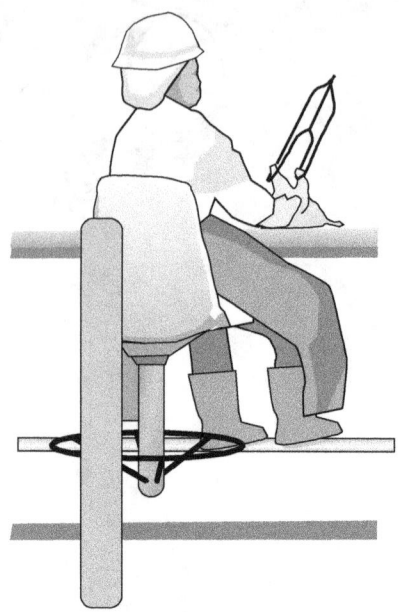

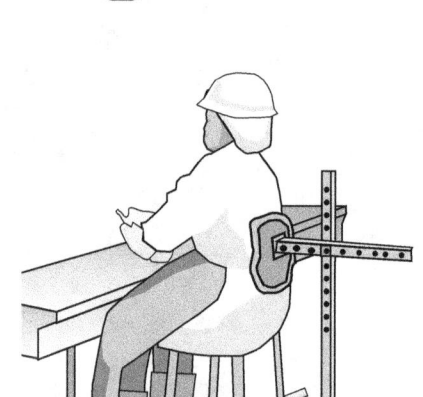

DESCRIPTION:

Seating and support devices for employees at fixed workstations to reduce prolonged periods of standing. These may vary depending on the nature of the workstation. A chair or stool may be appropriate for off-line processes where there is limited movement. Sit/stand stools or lean bars may be more appropriate for line positions where there is need to reach, grab, and throw product.

WHEN TO USE:

At all appropriate stationary sitting and standing positions.

POINTS TO REMEMBER:

- Selecting the most appropriate support device promotes neutral body postures and reduces fatigue during seated, sit/stand, and standing tasks.
- The use of these devices should not result in extended forward or elevated reaching, bending, or trunk twisting.

Recommendations for Chairs:

- The chair should be adjustable to accommodate both the task being performed and the size of the worker.
- Tall chairs should include a mechanism for mounting and dismounting such as a footrail. Prolonged use of a footrail may obstruct bloodflow to the leg; therefore, a footrest should be provided for long duration use.
- Footrest surface area should be deep enough to support the whole foot and large enough to allow some sideward and forward movement for position changes. Position the footrest to prevent an excessively bent or straight knee posture. A slight open angle of the knee is preferred. Height adjustability of the footrest is preferred. Select an adjustment mechanism that does not result in posture, force, or sanitation problems. Teach workers when and how to make proper adjustments.
- Where height adjustability is not provided, select at least two fixed-height footrests to accommodate the smallest height person. Recess the upper footrest slightly so it does not become an obstacle for the lower footrest.
- Seat pan depth should support the thigh but should not touch the back of the knee.
- Seat angle should support the thigh evenly.
- The backrest should be height-adjustable and large enough to support the upper and lower back. The shape of the backrest should provide support for the inward curve of the low back.
- Armrests are seldom appropriate for hand-intensive tasks and they may interfere with task requirements. If provided, the armrests should be adjustable for height and width.

Recommendations for Sit-Stand Stools:

- A high stool or angled seat provides a surface on which the worker can lean, shift weight, and change trunk angle.
- With an angled seat, only leaning can occur. With a flat seat, the worker may plant one foot on the floor and rest the other thigh on the seat for support.
- The base should be fixed so that it does not move unintentionally.

Recommendations for Backrests or Leaning Devices:

- Another type of leaning device is an independent back support without a seat that is stationary, stable, and height-adjustable. It should provide adequate support for both the upper and lower back. Provide clearance for required cleaning and sanitation.
- Position the device to prevent forward trunk bending.
- Ensure clearance behind devices so as not to obstruct passage of other employees walking past the workstation.

WORKSTATIONS - Rework

DESCRIPTION:
Designated workstation or work area designed for evisceration and cutting of poultry that cannot be processed at the standard production line.

WHEN TO USE:
For damaged birds that require extra handling to remove unwanted parts.

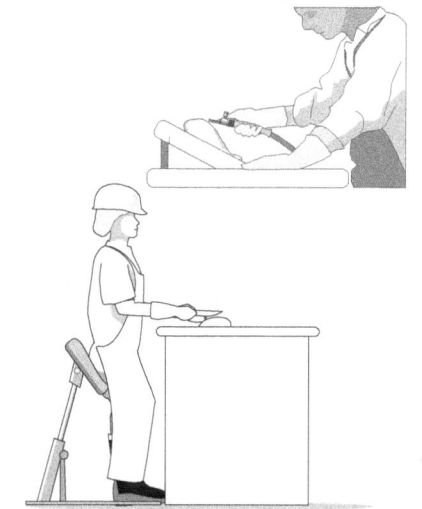

POINTS TO REMEMBER:
- Transporting these poultry parts away from the normal processing line allows the worker adequate time to closely examine and remove unwanted parts.
- Use pneumatic or mechanical cutting devices where appropriate to minimize hand forces.
- The use of fixtures and/or a slightly forward-slanted table may be appropriate to position poultry parts so that work can be completed using neutral body postures.
- May be used as an alternative work area or part of rotation plan since work is self-paced and slower than conventional assembly lines.

DESCRIPTION:
Work surfaces or work stands that adjust to fit the worker and the task performed.

WHEN TO USE:
At all workstations.

POINTS TO REMEMBER:
- Proper workstation height minimizes excessive forward trunk-bending and lifting of the arms when cleaning, preparing, and packing whole birds and poultry parts.
- Proper hand height improves comfort by reducing wrist deviation, forward reaches and elbow bending.
- Tilting the cutting block can reduce bending of the wrist.

Table height recommendations:
- Employees should have height-adjustable work tables or height-adjustable work stands so they can properly position themselves in relation to the work. Work surface height should attempt to minimize neck and torso bending and minimize, if possible, wrist deviation. Generally work surface should be:
  - slightly higher than elbow height for close visual inspection.
  - slightly below elbow height for low force manual tasks such as deboning or boxing. Table height should help accommodate neutral wrist postures. (Note: Table height may need to be lowered further to accommodate the height of a packing box.)
  - below elbow height, unless close visual inspection is required, for work requiring heavy force (e.g., some cutting or deboning).
- Powered adjustable height work surfaces that are positioned for use by individual workers can be spring-loaded or electrically powered by a motor.
- Work tables associated with conveyors can seldom be adjusted. These work surfaces should be designed for taller employees and should have standing platforms to accommodate shorter employees. Teach employees how and when to adjustable height. Provide adjustment controls that can be operated without causing a posture, force, or sanitation problem.

Standing work surface design recommendations:
- Provide height-adjustable standing platforms to reduce working with the elbows pulled away from the body.
- Lower input and takeaway conveyors and chutes to prevent reaching above shoulder height.
- Provide adequate clearance so workers can take a step sideways along the conveyor when necessary and so the whole foot is supported when placed slightly forward or behind the body.
- A railing on the back edge of the platform may be added to reduce fall hazards. Provide a platform depth that allows egress passage behind employees when they are at their workstations.
- Provide non-slip flooring in areas that become wet or soiled with animal fat.
- Use perforated rather than slatted flooring where possible. Where slats are used, they should be flat and wide to minimize pressure points on the feet.
- Non-slip anti-fatigue mats that can be easily removed for cleaning may be added to solid floor for comfort.

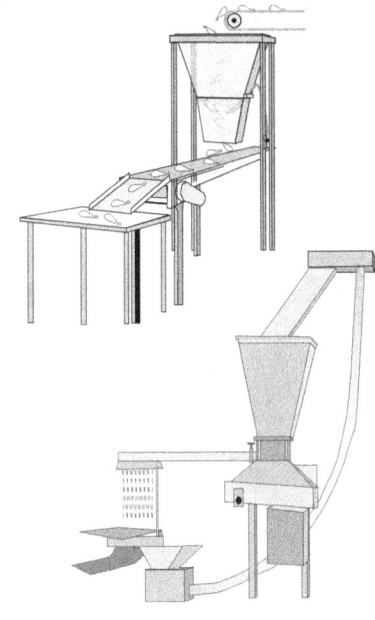

DESCRIPTION:

Hoppers are containers used to accumulate, hold and dispense contents into a machine, a new container, or onto a workstation through a restricted gate or using a screw-type auger mechanism. These facilitate the use of bulk loading and automated discrete transfer instead of manually loading, carrying, and emptying many individual boxes or bags. Augers use a screw-type device placed in a chute or trough to move and distribute items. An auger placed in a bulk storage container can remove a defined amount of product (depending on the size of screw) and move it to a new area where it can be deposited. Advantages of augers over other transport devices such as conveyor or tubs include controlled transfer from one place to another, especially of loose product moved up an incline, without lifting, shoveling, and carrying.

WHEN TO USE:

When accumulation and dispensing or transfer of product or other items is required.

POINTS TO REMEMBER:

- Hoppers with discharge chutes are generally preferred for dispensing larger unitized objects such as poultry parts, whereas augers are generally preferred for loose product such as ice, spices, and tenderizers in predetermined quantity to match recipe or packaging units.
- Hoppers are loaded from the top of the unit and have a gate to drop smaller portions in bulk or pre-measured quantities, whereas augers have screw-type mechanisms that can discreetly move smaller portions from bulk containers, such as a tub, hopper, or bin, and dispense those portions in pre-measured quantities.
- Operation can be automatic or employee-initiated with activation controls located to avoid reaching and bending.
- May replace the need for manual portioning by scooping or shoveling, especially for ice.
- To load hoppers and avoid additional lifting, consider devices such as mechanical lifters, dumpers, augers, and conveyors.

DESCRIPTION:
Wheeled devices designed to transport materials.

WHEN TO USE:
For transporting containers of whole birds, bird parts, processed meats, waste products, or supplies between work areas.

POINTS TO REMEMBER:
- A small lip around the edges of shelves on carts is helpful to prevent items from slipping off.
- Ensure that the top stack height does not obstruct vision.
- Optimal shelf height range should be between knuckle (with arms at side) and shoulder height.
- Pushing is preferred to pulling.
- Balance loads and keep loads within manufacturer's weight restrictions.
- Handles that are vertical allow all workers to place their hands at optimal positions on the handle so they can push with hands at about chest elbow height. Some horizontal adjustment allows placement of hands at shoulder width apart. A swing-out design may be useful to improve access.

- Manually pushed carts and hand trucks should have full bearing wheels made of a material designed for the floor surface in the facility. Generally, solid hard wheels are preferable on concrete or other hand surfaces. Pneumatic wheels perform better on rough uneven surfaces. Wheeled devices that will be used on ramped surfaces should have hand brakes that are easy to operate.
- Wheeled devices should have brakes or docking areas that prevent unintentional movement of the cart or hand truck when left unattended or when loading.
- Larger wheels are generally easier to push. Rear swivel and front fixed wheel design improves ease of pushing and steering, especially if the cart is long. In some designs, a third set of non-swivel wheels is placed centrally to add stability and improve ease of turning.
- Heavily loaded carts should have power-assisted drive mechanisms. Generally, a well maintained cart on a smooth flat surface should be loaded to no more than 500 pounds if it is to be moved manually.
- Carts may be designed for general use or for specialized applications. Specialty carts that have contours or clamps to hold specific supplies (e.g., rolls of plastic) may be designed to aid in supply transfer directly to the machine or work surface that uses that product.
- Large bucket-type containers on carts should have an angled front to allow tipping for removal of contents (e.g., utility tilt trucks).
- Devices such as pallet jacks, lift tables and pallet stands should be height-adjustable and rotate to allow parts and supplies to be positioned at proper working heights and orientation. They may be used in conjunction with staging for vacuum systems and a variety of workstation designs. These devices improve working posture by reducing unnecessary bending and reaching.
- Pallet jacks may be manual or motorized. The motorized version is preferred for frequent or long-distance travel.

DESCRIPTION:
Rack and shelf design to optimize manual access.

WHEN TO USE:
Shelf systems can be configured to minimize excessive lifting, carrying, and awkward postures associated with storage of any item used or produced at a workstation.

POINTS TO REMEMBER:
- For items that will be manually lifted, shelf height should be from approximately knuckle (with arms at side) to shoulder height. Store heavy and frequently used items in this range. Storage of lightweight and infrequently used items above and below this range is acceptable. Labels on shelves may help to quickly and easily identify materials to be lifted or carried.
- Bulk packages of supplies that are transported by mechanical devices can be stacked and stored as needed. However, once packages are opened and removed manually, placement on shelves should follow the recommendations listed above.
- Be aware that the deeper shelves are front to back, the harder they may be to access both visually and manually. It may be necessary to increase the vertical distance between deeper shelves to make it easier to see and reach items placed on them.

DESCRIPTION:
Vacuum systems for lifting and transport of materials.

WHEN TO USE:
Vacuum systems can be used for lifting and transporting poultry parts, boxes of product, spice bags, ice, and other materials. Applications of vacuum systems include:

- Vacuum systems can be attached to a lifting device. The vacuum is used to secure the load to the lifting device and the device is used to provide an assist for lifting and placement of items onto racks or pallets for storage or transport.
- Vacuum systems can be connected to chutes or transport tubes which use an air stream to transport lighter individual poultry parts.

POINTS TO REMEMBER:
- Vacuum entry points can be placed at individual work areas to gather product for transport to chillers or other holding areas for further processing or packaging.
- Vacuum systems can be designed specifically to handle internal transport of hearts, livers, gizzards, and necks from harvesting area for further processing.
- There are a wide variety of attachments that can be used with vacuum lifting systems. These are especially useful for odd sized and shaped product.

DESCRIPTION:
Mechanical systems such as roller-driven sheets of textured fabric or suspended shackles/hooks that continually move product.

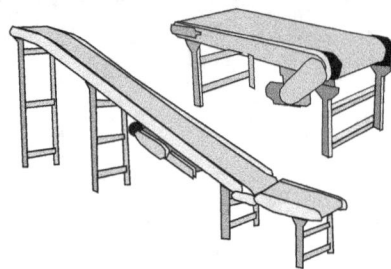

WHEN TO USE:
Replaces carrying of product around the plant. Moves product between the various processing stations.

POINTS TO REMEMBER:
- Ensure that mechanical equipment, conveyor sides, or supports do not impede access to product. Workers should be able to get close to the product without bending forward.
- Overhead conveyors should be designed so that the worker can grasp birds without reaching higher than mid-chest level. This can be accomplished by lowering the line or providing height-adjustable access for employees at their work area.
- Belt conveyors should be installed so that workers can grasp birds or bird parts while keeping their elbows close to the torso. The conveyor speed should allow sufficient time for the task being performed.
- Conveyors can be designed to reorient birds or bird parts.

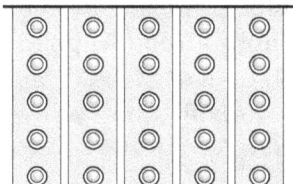

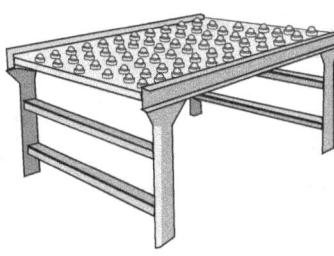

DESCRIPTION:
Tabletop or work surface embedded with rollers or ball bearings which allow product to be turned or repositioned. The rollers or ball bearings reduce friction and force when sliding items.

WHEN TO USE:
Recommended for transporting and repositioning boxes, bins, and other containers over relatively short distances.

POINTS TO REMEMBER:
- Rollers are preferred for transport in a linear direction whereas ball bearings are preferred when change of direction is required.
- Pushing or sliding containers eliminates lifting and carrying that can be strenuous to the hands, arms, and back.
- Appropriate for product in containers, but not loose parts due to sanitation issues.

ADDITIONAL SOURCES OF INFORMATION

The following training materials for the Poultry Processing Industry were developed under Susan Harwood training grants: "Safe and Secure: Safety Training Series" by the Telamon Corporation (2010), "Safety in Meatpacking, Poultry Processing and Food Processing" by the United Food and Commercial Workers International Union (2010), and "Sanitation Worker Safety and Health in the Poultry Industry" by the Georgia Tech Applied Research Corporation (2007). All of these materials can be found on the OSHA web site at: www.osha. gov/dte/grant_materials.

REFERENCES

(1) National Research Council and Institute of Medicine. *Musculoskeletal Disorders and the Workplace — Low Back and Upper Extremities.* National Academy of Sciences. Washington, DC: National Academies Press. 2001.

(2) *Musculoskeletal Disorders and Workplace Factors: A Critical Review of Epidemiologic Evidence for Work-Related Musculoskeletal Disorders of the Neck, Upper Extremity, and Low Back.* Cincinnati, OH: U.S. Department of Health and Human Services, Public Health Service, Centers for Disease Control and Prevention, National Institute for Occupational Safety and Health, DHHS. 1997. (NIOSH Publication No. 97-141.)

(3) Poultry Industry Task Force. The Medical Ergonomics Training Program: A Guide for the Poultry Industry. (OSHA Docket GE2003-2, Exhibit 4-2.) 1986.

(4) U.S. Department of Labor, Occupational Safety and Health Administration. *Ergonomics Program Management Guidelines for Meatpacking Plants.* Reprinted 1993.

(5) Bureau of Labor Statistics. U.S. Department of Labor, Table SNR12. Highest incidence rates of total nonfatal occupational illness cases, 2012. http://www.bls.gov/iif/oshwc/osh/os/ostb3580.pdf; accessed 12/4/2013.

(6) BLS data query system for Case and Demographic Incidence Rates Profiles; BLS data, 2012. http://data.bls.gov/gqt/InitialPage; accessed 12/4/2013.

(7) BLS data query system for Case and Demographic Numbers Profiles; BLS data, 2012. http://data.bls.gov/gqt/InitialPage; accessed 12/4/2013.

(8) NIOSH. Musolin K, Ramsey JG, Wassell JT, Mueller C, *Musculoskeletal Disorders and Traumatic Injuries Among Employees at a Poultry Processing Plant.* Interim Report HHE No. 2012-0125. April 2013.

(9) Cartwright MS, Walker FO, Blocker JN, Schulz MR, Arcury TA, Grzywacz JG, Mora D, Chen H, Marin AJ, Quandt SA. The prevalence of carpal tunnel syndrome in Latino poultry-processing workers and other Latino manual workers. *J Occup Environ Med,* 2012; 54(2):198-201.

(10) NIOSH. Hazard evaluation and technical assistance report: Longmont Turkey Processors, Inc., Longmont, CO: U.S. Department of Health and Human Services, Public Health Service, Centers for Disease Control and Prevention, National Institute for Occupational Safety and Health, NIOSH HETA Report No. 86-505-1885. 1988.

(11) NIOSH. Hazard evaluation and technical assistance report: Cargill Poultry Division, Buena Vista, GA: U.S. Department of Health and Human Services, Public Health Service, Centers for Disease Control and Prevention, National Institute for Occupational Safety and Health, NIOSH HETA Report No. 89-251-1997. November 1989.

(12) Reports of OSHA site visits to poultry processing facilities. (OSHA Docket GE2003-2, Exhibit 4-5.)

(13) Jones, Ronald J. Corporate Ergonomics Program of a Large Poultry Processor. *AIHA Journal* (58). February 1997.

(14) GAO. Workplace Health and Safety: Safety in the meat and poultry industry, while improving, could be further strengthened. U.S. Government Accountability Office, GAO-05-96. 2005.

(15) *Elements of Ergonomics Programs: A Primer Based on Evaluations of Musculoskeletal Disorders.* Cincinnati, OH: U.S. Department of Health and Human Services, Public Health Service, Centers for Disease Control and Prevention, National Institute for Occupational Safety and Health, DHHS. (NIOSH Publication No. 97-117). 1997.

(16) Silverstein B and Evanoff B. Chapter 16 – Musculoskeletal Disorders. In Levy, Barry S.; Wegman, David H.; Baron, Sherry L. *Occupational and Environmental Health: Recognizing and Preventing Disease and Injury* (6th Edition). Cary, NC, USA: Oxford University Press, USA, 2010. Pgs. 349-351.

WORKERS' RIGHTS

Under OSHA law, workers are entitled to working conditions that do not pose a risk of serious harm. To help assure a safe and healthful workplace, the law provides workers with the right to:

- File a confidential complaint with OSHA to have their workplace inspected.
- Receive information and training about hazards, methods to prevent harm, and the OSHA standards that apply to their workplace. The training must be done in a language and vocabulary workers can understand.
- Receive copies of records of work-related injuries and illnesses that occur in their workplace.
- Receive copies of the results from tests and monitoring done to find and measure hazards in their workplace.
- Receive copies of their workplace medical records.
- Participate in an OSHA inspection and speak in private with the inspector.
- File a complaint with OSHA if they have been retaliated against by their employer as the result of requesting an inspection or using any of their other rights under the OSH Act.
- File a complaint if punished or retaliated against for acting as a "whistleblower" under the 21 additional federal laws for which OSHA has jurisdiction.

For more information, visit OSHA's Workers' Rights page at www.osha.gov/workers.html.

OSHA ASSISTANCE, SERVICES AND PROGRAMS

OSHA offers free compliance assistance to employers and workers. Several OSHA programs and services can help employers identify and correct job hazards, as well as improve their injury and illness prevention program.

Establishing an Injury and Illness Prevention Program

The key to a safe and healthful work environment is a comprehensive injury and illness prevention program.

Injury and illness prevention programs are systems that can substantially reduce the number and severity of workplace injuries and illnesses, while reducing costs to employers. Thousands of employers across the United States already manage safety using illness and injury prevention programs, and OSHA believes that all employers can and should do the same. Thirty-four states have requirements or voluntary guidelines for workplace injury and illness prevention programs. Most successful injury and illness prevention programs are based on a common set of key elements. These include management leadership, worker participation, hazard identification, hazard prevention and control, education and training,

and program evaluation and improvement. Visit OSHA's illness and injury prevention program web page at www.osha.gov/dsg/topics/safetyhealth for more information.

Compliance Assistance Specialists

OSHA has compliance assistance specialists throughout the nation located in most OSHA offices. Compliance assistance specialists can provide information to employers and workers about OSHA standards, short educational programs on specific hazards or OSHA rights and responsibilities, and information on additional compliance assistance resources. For more details, visit www.osha.gov/dcsp/compliance_assistance/cas.html or call 1-800-321-OSHA [6742] to contact your local OSHA office.

Free On-site Safety and Health Consultation Services for Small Business

OSHA's On-site Consultation Program offers free and confidential advice to small and medium-sized businesses in all states across the country, with priority given to high-hazard worksites. Each year, responding to requests from small employers looking to create or improve their safety and health management programs, OSHA's On-site Consultation Program conducts over 29,000 visits to small business worksites covering over 1.5 million workers across the nation.

On-site consultation services are separate from enforcement and do not result in penalties or citations. Consultants from state agencies or universities work with employers to identify workplace hazards, provide advice on compliance with OSHA standards, and assist in establishing safety and health management programs.

For more information, to find the local On-site Consultation office in your state, or to request a brochure on Consultation Services, visit www.osha.gov/consultation, or call 1-800-321-OSHA [6742].

Under the consultation program, certain exemplary employers may request participation in OSHA's **Safety and Health Achievement Recognition Program (SHARP)**. Eligibility for participation includes, but is not limited to, receiving a full-service, comprehensive consultation visit, correcting all identified hazards and developing an effective safety and health management program. Worksites that receive SHARP recognition are exempt from programmed inspections during the period that the SHARP certification is valid.

Cooperative Programs

OSHA offers cooperative programs under which businesses, labor groups and other organizations can work cooperatively with OSHA. To find out more about any of the following programs, visit www.osha.gov/dcsp/compliance_assistance/index_programs.html.

Strategic Partnerships and Alliances

The OSHA Strategic Partnerships (OSP) provides the opportunity for OSHA to partner with employers, workers, professional or trade associations, labor organizations, and/or other interested stakeholders. OSHA Strategic Partnerships are formalized through unique agreements designed to encourage, assist, and recognize partner efforts to eliminate serious hazards and achieve model workplace safety and health practices. Through the Alliance Program,

OSHA works with groups committed to worker safety and health to prevent workplace fatalities, injuries and illnesses by developing compliance assistance tools and resources to share with workers and employers, and educate workers and employers about their rights and responsibilities.

Voluntary Protection Programs (VPP)

The VPP recognize employers and workers in private industry and federal agencies who have implemented effective safety and health management programs and maintain injury and illness rates below the national average for their respective industries. In VPP, management, labor, and OSHA work cooperatively and proactively to prevent fatalities, injuries, and illnesses through a system focused on: hazard prevention and control, worksite analysis, training, and management commitment and worker involvement.

Occupational Safety and Health Training

The OSHA Training Institute in Arlington Heights, Illinois, provides basic and advanced training and education in safety and health for federal and state compliance officers, state consultants, other federal agency personnel and private sector employers, workers, and their representatives. In addition, 27 OSHA Training Institute Education Centers at 42 locations throughout the United States deliver courses on OSHA standards and occupational safety and health issues to thousands of students a year.

For more information on training, contact the OSHA Directorate of Training and Education, 2020 Arlington Heights Road, Arlington Heights, IL 60005; call 1-847-297-4810; or visit www.osha.gov.

OSHA Educational Materials

OSHA has many types of educational materials in English, Spanish, Vietnamese and other languages available in print or online. These include:

- Brochures/booklets that cover a wide variety of job hazards and other topics;
- Fact Sheets, which contain basic background information on safety and health hazards;
- Guidance documents that provide detailed examinations of specific safety and health issues;

- Online Safety and Health Topics pages;
- Posters;
- Small, laminated QuickCards™ that provide brief safety and health information; and
- *QuickTakes*, OSHA's free, twice-monthly online newsletter with the latest news about OSHA initiatives and products to assist employers and workers in finding and preventing workplace hazards. To sign up for *QuickTakes* visit OSHA's web site at www.osha.gov and click on *QuickTakes* at the top of the page.

To view materials available online or for a listing of free publications, visit OSHA's web site at www.osha.gov. You can also call 1-800-321-OSHA [6742] to order publications.

OSHA's web site also has a variety of eTools. These include utilities such as expert advisors, electronic compliance assistance, videos and other information for employers and workers. To learn more about OSHA's safety and health tools online, visit www.osha.gov.

NIOSH HEALTH HAZARD EVALUATION PROGRAM

Getting Help with Health Hazards

The National Institute for Occupational Safety and Health (NIOSH) is a federal agency that conducts scientific and medical research on workers' safety and health. At no cost to employers or workers, NIOSH can help identify health hazards and recommend ways to reduce or eliminate those hazards in the workplace through its Health Hazard Evaluation (HHE) Program.

Workers, union representatives and employers can request a NIOSH HHE. An HHE is often requested when there is a higher than expected rate of a disease or injury in a group of workers. These situations may be the result of an unknown cause, a new hazard, or a mixture of sources. To request a NIOSH Health Hazard Evaluation go to www.cdc.gov/niosh/hhe/request.html. To find out more about the Health Hazard Evaluation Program:

- Call (513) 841-4382, or to talk to a staff member in Spanish, call (513) 841-4439; or
- Send an email to HHERequestHelp@cdc.gov.

OSHA REGIONAL OFFICES

Region I
Boston Regional Office
(CT*, ME, MA, NH, RI, VT*)
JFK Federal Building, Room E340
Boston, MA 02203
(617) 565-9860 (617) 565-9827 Fax

Region II
New York Regional Office
(NJ*, NY*, PR*, VI*)
201 Varick Street, Room 670
New York, NY 10014
(212) 337-2378 (212) 337-2371 Fax

Region III
Philadelphia Regional Office
(DE, DC, MD*, PA, VA*, WV)
The Curtis Center
170 S. Independence Mall West
Suite 740 West
Philadelphia, PA 19106-3309
(215) 861-4900 (215) 861-4904 Fax

Region IV
Atlanta Regional Office
(AL, FL, GA, KY*, MS, NC*, SC*, TN*)
61 Forsyth Street, SW, Room 6T50
Atlanta, GA 30303
(678) 237-0400 (678) 237-0447 Fax

Region V
Chicago Regional Office
(IL*, IN*, MI*, MN*, OH, WI)
230 South Dearborn Street
Room 3244
Chicago, IL 60604
(312) 353-2220 (312) 353-7774 Fax

Region VI
Dallas Regional Office
(AR, LA, NM*, OK, TX)
525 Griffin Street, Room 602
Dallas, TX 75202
(972) 850-4145 (972) 850-4149 Fax
(972) 850-4150 FSO Fax

Region VII
Kansas City Regional Office
(IA*, KS, MO, NE)
Two Pershing Square Building
2300 Main Street, Suite 1010
Kansas City, MO 64108-2416
(816) 283-8745 (816) 283-0547 Fax

Region VIII
Denver Regional Office
(CO, MT, ND, SD, UT*, WY*)
Cesar Chavez Memorial Building
1244 Speer Boulevard, Suite 551
Denver, CO 80204
(720) 264-6550 (720) 264-6585 Fax

Region IX
San Francisco Regional Office
(AZ*, CA*, HI*, NV*, and American Samoa,
Guam and the Northern Mariana Islands)
90 7th Street, Suite 18100
San Francisco, CA 94103
(415) 625-2547 (415) 625-2534 Fax

Region X
Seattle Regional Office
(AK*, ID, OR*, WA*)
300 Fifth Avenue, Suite 1280
Seattle, WA 98104
(206) 757-6700 (206) 757-6705 Fax

* These states and territories operate their own OSHA-approved job safety and health plans and cover state and local government employees as well as private sector employees. The Connecticut, Illinois, New Jersey, New York and Virgin Islands programs cover public employees only. (Private sector workers in these states are covered by Federal OSHA). States with approved programs must have standards that are identical to, or at least as effective as, the Federal OSHA standards.

Note: To get contact information for OSHA area offices, OSHA-approved state plans and OSHA consultation projects, please visit us online at www.osha.gov or call us at 1-800-321-OSHA (6742).

HOW TO CONTACT OSHA

For questions or to get information or advice, to report an emergency, report a fatality or catastrophe, order publications, sign up for OSHA's e-newsletter *QuickTakes*, or to file a confidential complaint, contact your nearest OSHA office, visit www.osha.gov or call OSHA at 1-800-321-OSHA (6742), TTY 1-877-889-5627.

For assistance, contact us.
We are OSHA. We can help.